daniel berrigan

prison poems

daniel berrigan

prison poems

foreword by philip berrigan

unicorn press

Second printing, 1982

Assistance in the publication of this edition was received from the National Endowment for the Arts, a Federal Agency.

U N I C O R N   P R E S S

P.O. Box 3307, Greensboro, North Carolina 27402

Table of Contents

foreword

by

philip berrigan

As an introductory statement to my brother's book of prison poems, I have been asked to respond to two questions, which I do with a sense of inadequacy, even ineptitude. First, what does it mean to be imprisoned with a Christian like Daniel Berrigan; secondly, how did prison impress these poems.

The two questions are really one. Dan, more than any person I've known, remained consistent through the action of Catonsville, through four months of living underground, culminating in nineteen months of painful and unpredictable lock-up. By consistent, I mean that he maintained a vision, a vision of non-violent resistance, a vision of community formation. But in a deeper sense, he held onto a vision that insisted upon life — its essential definitions, its prerogatives, its triumphs.

As I see it, one fundamental question occupied him: how does a human being live in the most intensely systematized version of non-life known to humanity? How does one maintain fidelity to God and to sisters and brothers when the overwhelming weight of culture, institutional religion, and official Statecraft locks one into unbelief and alienation?

As a resister — again, more consistently than any resister I have known — Dan lived in fidelity and compassion. His resistance in prison, his availability to all prisoners (Christian or otherwise), his fortitude under disappointment and bad health, his agonizing concern for Vietnamese, for Americans — for victims anywhere — displayed brilliantly what he believed. What he believed was obviously more important to him than his own life.

As he lived what he believed, so he wrote of what he believed. Writing was as integral to his life in prison as counseling, or rapping, or organizing, or listening to the anguish of a prison brother. That is why these poems, born of the grief and glory of prison life, are doorways to a great spirit. Like thousands in prison and out, I remain profoundly in his debt. I cannot explain this debt, but merely acknowledge it — and wonder at it.

prison poems

The Pearl of Great Price

Variety of responses here!
One walks the yard as though made of lucite
an expensive anatomical doll
lit up   ribboned like a Christmas tree –
or carrying his soul on his forehead
like a miner's lamp
searching out, eye to eye,
the rare el dorado lode of manhood.

Mostly, prisoners find it in themselves
to respect us. Something secreted
like the pearl the half-mad space cadet
sewed in his pants lining
for passage out of hell.
Some find it in their own craw, some
residue of dignity, unviolated
by the thumbs of the asshole brigade.
We're the mirrors then; recognition
artists, in the Greek sense: *know thyself.*

Mostly taken for granted.
Magic?   it folds up.
Mystery?   mainly it's making do
with clumsy grace, raising a paltry shelter,
swallowing what can't be changed,
whistling in the black box,
applying to affected parts (invariably
or by analogy, anal) the stinking
raw gum of Araby – black humor.
The principle: that which farts back, must be
alive. Or again: enough hate to let love
break through.

Jesus spoke with scorn
of the hireling! They come and go
dealers in human pelts and hooves

hating us and themselves, clutching for last resort
spouse, bank book, scrotum, never hearing
the purgatorial clanging to of dark
the clanging open
of hell hole day.

God himself, interest assumed, would have to
edge in close, were He
to whiff this cup – the lives of prisoners;
part sting, part nausea,
part horror vacui.
Nevertheless
the Spirit is poured abroad –
Zest in flatland;
poured out among the quaking
fat con artists,
their dolce vita foreclosed by the gimlet
eye of the Thin Man;
poured out among war resisters
those rasps and files
new as new steel, hurting as youth hurts
laid to the adamantine world;
poured out among druggies and dealers
black brown and not so beautiful
(the mud fouled yard through muddy eyeballs
shrieks, shrinks, paranoia.)

My mind reverts
to that pearl, lopsided
as a falling tear, a milky
unborn eye, sewn in the filthy seam
of a broken life.
The boy unspread it, a wad
of toilet paper, his hand like the broom end
of a scarecrow brain. Held it there
that midge of silence, after the last laugh

of the crazed universe.
Might buy it all back
might in the old stately sense "redeem" –
lying there in the wind-driven raw
wound of the mad innocent. All, all we had.
Snatched away in chains next day
never again seen.

Patience, Hard Virtue

Patience, tedious non Virtue
hangs around hangs around
Pantheon, cave of Aeolus
the last hour of Socrates
wherever the action is —
near hero, or near beer or
money laid on the slow horse
History, out of Time
(fool and money soon parted.)

He's waiting.   Outlasting
poverty programs, pogroms,
skins and their trade.
Hangs around.   Hangers-on sidle up
to stand beside.
Dumb animals, still
or raddled streams, straw,
stars, flowers that
transmogrify the show —

It seems to me when the Man
makes meat of us or less
the less is still the more;
the meat is greater heart;
cut to the bone, patience
outlasts the butcher's tool.

Hard, hard, no resolution:
the con's infernal whine,
the druggie's addled tongue,
intemperance, cowardice,
the monstrous world's mirror
held up to nature, held
corrective, cruel, exact
to our own face, day
after night, imposed

night upon sorrowing day.

The universe waits on us;
great patience on a lesser.
A prisoner's days run,
the weeks a slow drawn pain,
the years standing like stone.
Great nature doing time.
Hard time, easy time –
clobbering or tender hands
jack boots or juggernauts

"Consider the lilies –"
good news, good humor, grace.
I had rather so live, a few
brothers assailed, than mick-mock
whoring Caesar's strut.

Who pays, who renounces, who
makes that news anew?
unheard of news, heard now
seen now, touched now. I had rather –
but how descry it? My eyes
flare like a lamp in rain –

Hang around. Patience. Hear it:
The children live, the children
rise from My Lai ditch.

A Prayer to the Blessed Trinity

I'm locked into the sins of General Motors
My guts are in revolt at the culinary equivocations of
General Foods
Hang over me like an evil shekinah, the missiles of
General Electric.
Now we shall go from the Generals to the Particulars.
Father, Son, Holy Ghost
Let me shake your right hands in the above mentioned order.
Unmoved Motor, Food For Thought, Electric One.
I like you better than your earthly idols.
You seem honest and clear-minded and reasonably resolved
To make good on your promise.
Please: owe it to yourselves not less than to us,
Warn your people: beware of adulterations.

We Used to Meet for Classes. Sometimes It Was Ecstasy, Sometimes Blah

The big claims of the powerless are not notably more
                                  interesting
than the big claims of the powerful. The first inspire pity
   the others, fear. Together they make a parody
of the tragic. Now and again in our prisoners' class
   someone, a new arrival or a loquacious con man
takes over. Pushing his big claim up front
   a rickety cart laden with dubious "goods," slightly tainted
      virtuous side upward.
He would die, in sum, for this or that. (I forget what)
   Our fingers drum. The words of dead heroes
twitch in our hands like a struck face.

   Like torches stuck in the ground, a night encampment
an unwearied courage; thought plays, light and shadow
   cross
a mad general flays the air
A mad president charts, premises, promises.   A seductive
                               foreshortening
of the long march.
   "Take over – revolution – consciousness 3." Eyes cloud.
Have heard it all before, have heard it all
   before, heard it all, all before
before

In Prison, As Out, Time Is of the Essence

Methodical rampage
   Texans, conquistadors, empire builders!
No, teach my eyes to rejoice
in 1 sugaring unbudded tree, 1 star
   framed in a barred window, broad existence
narrowed to a keeper's eye. Gandhi and Jesus
   in time of prevarication, my teachers of honor.
Grow small, embrace in 2 arms, time grown small
   the nada of hermits and the friends of God.

A Survivor

Youngest of trees, the ancient ginkgo,
small as a heron, and fragile; doomed from its birth
(so it seemed) in the careless, spit-pocked yard.
There, of hundreds of lives, it was justly said,
no one damned or dared.
   The tree fell away to bare bones.
I gave it up with a shrug
such as, harried, one bestows
on a newsprint victim, a child, a woman of Vietnam.

Turn page; rage, burn.
In 3 weeks that forlorn thing
under the sun's gentle urging
fanned out, in delicate webbed finery.
It set all awry, uneasy, our
sardonic and settled glances, unseeing,
lackluster, loveless, giving up ghost.

Kermit

1 of those children of open spaces
        we used to transport by muleteam and covered wagon
1000 miles, 2000, at the drop of a gov't hint
        land for the landless –
    he's stuck here, like our history
            wagon tongue   Mules, bones
the great divide   the yawn of moral ennui
    Prison.   Busted for drugs.
This kid   wide grin   necromancer's big eyes
a mop of hair like home grown coonskin
        above all a joyous intemperate will
to walk with the wind & heat & miles
    of creation (those plague ridden winds   wasting heats
            macadam wastes) alas   America
He thinks day & night   (told me today)
    of finding "his place   his shack"
        1 ocean/freehold/acre/   hill / river /
    all in gentle conjunction   profusion untamed
        as seen offshore in the frame of a bosun's glass
by an explorer's crew

I watch him as a parent watches from shadows   face wet with
                                                        tears
    a premature infant's struggle   minute by minute
        for the world's blue air –
        make it!   or we all come down
in the vulgar trap shoot   the open season on man.
            O   america!
10:30 PM count   the cells close like a jaw
his hope   (mine) glimmers on
            we go
        in dream
        to our dream

Almost Everybody Is Dying Here: Only A Few Actually Make It

at 12:30 sharp
as though to underscore
some unassuageable grief
a man's head fell to one side
in the prison hospital.
No record of heart disease
a morning's weakness only. His neck went limp
in the pale March sunlight
like a wax man's.
his hands opened, a beggar's hesitant reach
before a rich man's shadow.
Near, there and
gone.

I Said No No

       i said: what you are doing
       is full as a cheese with the zeros
       of cunning rodents
he smiled from the maze   the smile
of a magic man
he was hand carved   wonderfully weathered
a sitting duck.   There was   (seeing that smile)
no help for it.
He was off to join the electric bones of Jeremiah
the wheat of the Pharaohs.
No help for it
a transmogrified high vaulter
by choice.
Clouds have no bones.
He rides and rains

Here Comes Another Rehabilitated Specimen: Watch Out

home from v. nam
jungle rot on his legs
stu- stu- stutter in his mouth
assault with intent to kill

creeping rot   stuttering tongue
assault w intent
    the statute of illimitation
    on foreign pelts and parts
    having no legal application
    2 American cits

the dead come home
bones in boxes
their lucky throw
& the peacock generals
screaming   rutting

& then this poor
bastard 4 whom
domestic engines
toll doomsday

unlucky & living

Outside
classics of their kind; bowed heads,
a suffocated inwardness, aimlessness.
    Except one.
Richie of the lank gold red hair, comic-strip face
    "mischievous American adolescent!" Except that between
    those innocuous stereotype frames, his true life lurks
fierce as a newly trapped animal, memory imprinted
    a bleeding tattoo of the lost wilderness.

I watch them, in a level place, pass a flower bed
    then shamble over a hill, half conscious, in search –
        something called "manhood."
        Not Richie. He stopped
    as though a few scant crocuses breaking ground
        were a fountainhead.
    O unincarcerated kid!   he went down on knee
        a boy racked with the filth and fury of life –
steel   concrete   foul talk   vapid food   empty heads
doughy hearts   hacks   lies   prearranged
    games of destruction   scents   trails   wet dreams   dry
                                                    tongues
        a thousand thirsts –
            he drank
    where the crocuses made a clear pool
        like flowers of fiery water.

            Obedient to the Great Yahoo
            gnawed into submission
        the others disappeared over the hill
    Counterfeit refreshment dulls the soul's thirst
lackaday lackaday lackaday onward –
        disappeared over the hill
    no plans for survival

DANIEL BERRIGAN   18

We Were Permitted to Meet Together in Prison to Prepare for Trial

yesterday, the usual stiff-necked shakedown
room possessions person – then
entered the seemly company,
fellow indicted and co-conspirators.
nuns, priests, friends
the inadmissible evidence of their lives
vivid as blowing flowers in a dustbin
(the big eye outside, the praying mantis),
word went around quietly; we have bread and wine!
that unwinking eye
glassing over with boredom
the mice in all seriousness played
the Jesus game.   a reading from Ezekiel
on the doomed city. Silence. Philip whispering over the bread
(a con, a magian), over the 'mt. dew' tin can.
we broke and passed the loaf, the furtive hands
of endangered animals.
my body given for you.   my blood outpoured.
indictable action!   as in the first instance
of vagrant Jesus, in whose flesh rumors and truth
collided; usual penalty, rigorously applied.

My friends, it is the savor of life
you passed to me; vines, the diminished loaf
lost hillsides where the sun
sets the grapes beating like a hive
of human hearts;   Cornell gorges, the distant sea
Block Island swung like a hammock from its moorings –
I come to myself
a beast in a shoe box
sport
of the king of the cats

Gamblers Anonymous

Odds are 400 to 1
we will not make it, no.
The President bets and bets
his dentures against it.   The warden
hedges his bets, adroit.
The convicts bet cigarettes.
The media bet their ass –
cool tubes and ads, a no no.
Soldiers in D.C. last week
threw away
like hot iron, their medals,
changing bets in midstream.
I read somewhere how someone
named Socrates bet and lost.
I bet he won, once.
Priests
commonly hedge their bets;
they praise the loser
Jesus, but their old age
is stacked as hell.
Well.   When we came here
and put on khaki and
sweated it out like spiders
an inch from the match flame,
the smart boys in Harrisburg
lined up at the teller's window,
emptied their pockets like mad.
They would pick us to pieces
like spiders, Phil and myself
and the other abettors and aiders.
Well.   I never lost my shirt
in a better cause.   Debtor's
jail is better than none.
I bet the national debt.

You Could Make a Song of It   A Dirge of It
A Heartbreaker of It

EVERYONE everyone in america
carries the war around with him
N. Mailer carries the war with him
2 inches on his waste line
B. Graham carries the war with him
at the root of his tongue   where the tongue forks out
left; turning a bible page
right; tasting the apples in the W. House garden
Bobby Seale carries the war with him
shackles to shoe laces.
The dying man in the cancer ward carries the war –
face to wall, kicked off the skids of the medicos.
The break-&-entry man   the acid freaks   the boy & girl
carry the war with them   Making love
is mortal sin   the warmakers march
the lovemakers die
Cardinals carry the war around, a sign of the †
Jews carry the war   the yarmulke sits
on the classified head of Kissinger
                                    The kids
toss a switchblade in the spring mud –
Territory!   they cry
carving the breathing earth like a turkey corpse.

O Danbury, To What Shall I Compare Thee?

Like coming up against testy Charon in a bad time
– or New York customs, en route from Hanoi, '68.
Notes stuffed in a paper bag.
Resolved: they'll have my life before
they have those words, scrawled in shelters
under their besotted bombs.

Some moments you're willing to die for,
die rather than have undone ...
I scrawl this, lights out, at a barred window.
Snow filigrees the April green.
Before they lay their cotton-picking paws on them
I'll eat these notes
alphabetize with good news
my prophetic guts.

Tulips in the Prison Yard

Many poets, believe me, could do better by your
sovereign beauty, your altogether subtle
transfiguration of blank nature –
so winds, nights, sunlight
colorless wraiths, are drawn into
what can only be called a "new game."
Well.   I will not glory
in infirmity.   Yeats, Wordsworth would look once
breathe deeply, sharpen their quills,
with a flourish pluck you from time.
But.
You are jail-yard blooms, you wear bravery with a difference.
You are born here will die here;
making you, by excess of suffering
and transfiguration of suffering, ours.

I see prisoners pass
in the dead spur of spring, before you show face

Are you their glancing tears
the faces of wives and children, the yin yang of hearts
to fro like hanged necks
perpetual cruelty, absurdity?

The prisoners
pass and pass; shades of men, pre-men,
khaki ghosts, shame, futility.
Between smiles, between reason for smiles, between
life as fool's pace and life as celebrant's flame –
aeons.
Yet, thank you.   Against the whips
of ignorant furies, the slavish pieties of judas priests
you stand, a first flicker in the brain's soil, the precursor
of judgment.

Dawn might be, man may be
or
spelling it out in the hand's palm
of a blind mute

God is fire, is love.

We Will Now Hear the Word of God from Each of Our Beloved Chaplains

1.
Rev stump is   believe it or not   for real
as a stump to a grown tree
so he to the verdant gospel
this corpulent burgher   this fictitious
rubbery stamp   Stump
a huckster's   a hack's gospel
Stump   wormwood   miles of smiles

2.
the priest   an irish caricature   wheels up
in his cadillac each a.m. an alderman
to a cobbler's funeral   we   the dead faces
his asperges hisses on   have yet
like Lazarus in hell
one cold Christian curse
bestowal, blessing

One Prisoner Was Driven Mad:
Let This Be a Lesson

Every symbol to which attaches
exact metaphysical resonance
is by necessity physical at the first.
If the lorn boy prisoner
streams and wavers like a spineless flag before our
horrified eyes,   it is because
he grabs and tightens in a fist
the scrotum of unbelievers
like us,
and faster holds
then the newly hung nylon pennant
big
as a stolen bedspread
on July 4th, 3 long prison days ago
proclaiming like Betsy Ross or Penelope;
Uncle Ulysses that far-darting uxorious spirit
is home; safe but unavailable
being mad.

Night time, the boy drinks the jughead moon
like a moonshine into his jugular
over his left shoulder
(3 big cops keep watch).   Shock treatments
sharpen his cunning.   Passing the fuzz
he jacks up his pants, breathes deep
like Charlie Chaplin, a shuffling tramp's
survival run.

In the presence of, say, an offshore fleet
it is advisable that natives show a low profile.
800 men per 2 acres of compound
may not be a generous slice of paradisaical wilderness;
still, given the 24 hour lock-up of certain federal facilities
a vivid scene of relative slavery
is staked formally in consciousness.
One young Panther put it:

Coming to Danbury after 10 years in other joints I blinked hard.
The nearest thing this nigger ever knew
to being free.

Likewise.   Life, liberty
and the pursuit of niggers, to any skin
grown wise in the successive sheep dips
of jail, jail and jail;
strictly relative.   Yes.
One's brain is pierced as though with the arrows of lilliput
by the mystical reality –
a few blades of grass, a tough stemmed tatterdemalion
flower.   Multum in parvo.
John Colton's guitar bears us aloft
(a summer evening, a vanquishing angel) by hair of head.
Though we swore, singly, repeatedly, to cling
to here and now, at whatever cost;
the past drowns us, past all rescue.
O my sister the sea,
My brother, fair land, what might
have been.   Air, fire, what we together –

8 O'Clock Morning Scene

a crowded car-load
of expertise

disgorges each A.M.
in the compound

running like beetles
each 2 his bureau

briefcases bulging
foreheads furrowed

mockups   motivations
instruments   lobotomies

up pills   down pills
blueprints   fingerprints

funny funny
a sparrow stretches

a wing   a leg   yawns
in the dawn light

nothing ever happens
here

Socrates

"Is there someone who understands
human and political virtue?"
I sit on Connecticut ice
October ice in the offing.
An old man argues his case
staff in hand, thumping
the noble ground
where human and political virtue
first arose.

Bad news, bad.
The Weathermen bomb at the wake
of the dead republic.
Rabbit calls good night
between the bars (grass: 2 yrs. for possession)
The grass thrives on the grave
of the suicidal republic.   The bars slide
scissors or jaw, into place.

Billy Bones

Limped into our dustbin "library"
just arrived in chains from Baltimore jail,
galled like a work horse –
no supper, no medication, hurt, famished
but "wanting"
(sublime principle in play – first things first
he burns in the mind as most burn in the crotch or belly)
"anything by Fanon, Marx, Che, etc.?"
I did a double take.
In the old monastery days the gyrovague monk, on return
from excursion beyond cloister
always visited the chapel first, before even
seeking the abbot's blessing.

First things first.
One can limp on a galled foot
know hunger and pain and rage
(black, a prisoner)
and yet sip on occasion a rare elixir
of the servant sovereign mind
even as behind one, time and its termites
consume bestially *el camino real*
and that tide
(thesis antithesis
to the mind's moon)
surges back, lover
to loved body.

A Typical 6:00 P.M. in the Fun House

He yelled *count finished!*   The machinery
swings back on its demented elbow.   We are stars or cattle
or the 16 winds or nest eggs or Fort Knox or quintuplets.
Some days my brain burns
a loaded circuit, with the massed burden of it all,
the bad news funneled into the dark tunnel
a raging train, a stinking herd –
7 layers of Sodom on the spirit.
Other days I make it,
counting like prayer beads, the hours dropped or palmed.
A lotus sprouts in the privy's filth.
The small tree outside, unfit for a man's dead weight, breathes,
hang on!

The Risen Tin Can

1.
Toward the rear end of the prison graveyard
   stands a frantic caterwauling machine that flattens tin cans.
Its iron flail beats the air to death
   even when no forage intervenes.
Let us consider as poets do, the rightful synecdoche of the
                                                situation.
   We prisoners are so to speak, tin cans
emptied of surprise, color, seed, heartbeat, pity, pitch, frenzy
   molasses, nails, ecstasy, etc., etc.
destined to be whiffed and tumbled into elements of flatland
   recycled, dead men's bones, dead souls –

Now the opposite of all this is the shudder and drumming feet
   of the risen tin can
over the hill, into the sunrise
   The tin can contains, grows wings, he writes poetry!

This is the year of the RISEN TIN CAN, in the Vietnamese sense.
   REVOLUTION REFUSAL REBUTTAL POETRY.
When I was a tin can I thought like a tin can I looked like a tin
                                                can I
   spoke like a tin can
now that I am a man I have put away the things of a tin can
   NEMPE
tin armaments tin hearts tin bells rin-tin-tin gross national tin
   American tin

No.
   It is expedient·that the glory of God be not
melted smelted milled rolled.
   It is required that mere men
even though with hanging head and drooping codpiece
   persuaded in contrariety to nature
of the intrinsic genetic inferiority

solar surfaced
   and O so cheap definitive solution
of TIN –

It is expedient
   that mere men and women prevail
in face of the Idol of Scissors Alley
   that hundred pincered crustacean can-and-man opener.

But I digress.
   The unforgivable sin against the unholy spirit
is the metamorphosis of tin
   into manhood.
Of which one instance: the writing of a poem.
   Shaking of foundations!   It is not to be borne
that sounding and tinkling tin
   unzipped, emptied of its regal redoutable guts brains gore
should arise to the phoenix form of the twice born.
Celebrate it!   An ivory stick on the Ethiopian drumhead
   the sweet tactile frenzy of B. B. King.
The puma's maeeeoooow of a steel band
   catgut reborn!   tin renascent!   us resurrected!

E contra
   the Neanderthal triumph of the century beyond reasonable
doubt is *Homo Danburiensis*

On the one hand
   the starched ars and starved brain of the cosseted correctionist
barking violations of the penny ante whipping out his tape
measure against the turds of the circus flea.
Then
   the raddled crook, unselfknowledgeable as an ass's elbow,
rounding the dice, squaring the roulette, night and day stuffing
his kicked tail into his parched mouth. Prayer; *O keep me from
Chrissake awakening!*

It is recounted in the old legends that a child came unannounced among the uncopacetic beasts who thereupon discovered unlikely good things in one another, and wrath laid aside, fed slept, foraged, wandered together, claw to fleece, tooth to feather.

The moral by gentle implication; the great Braggart and Beast himself, in comparison with whose ravenings the bestiality of beasts is a rare and mystic dance, might one day make peace as he perennially has made war.

Meantime the claims of the kingdom of death are beyond doubt total. They totalize and mobilize Unman for their surrogate. Henceforth in tribute to the GREAT PRETENDER, one must walk on garbage, feed on ugliness, break stones by day and grind his molars by night.

His keepers march like articulated tin can sandwich men parading the First Command of the Lost Way; BE LIKE ME!

But

Let a blade of grass intervene, a vagrant lustful loving frenetic stammer arise in one; let him remember his lost friends, the cords of Adam, let a single bird cross his starved sight –

Let a single countervailing voice, color, feeling, sound –

All is undone

The sweet world is suddenly at hand, a NECESSARY ANGEL;
BE UNLIKE CONNECT I AM THE WAY FREE EVERYONE
SHANTI SHANTI

Dear friends,
the Great Amortizer is at the door, syringe in hand.

He parts his face like a dead sea
into: benevolence or murder.

When he looks benevolent he means murder
When he looks murderous he means business
Business is good; you or someone else; viz –
He freezes your rent, he is burning someone's hut
He cures your cancer, he is filling his germ bottles

DANIEL BERRIGAN   34

He worships on Sunday   Buddhists die for it.
   This is called Caesar's karma.   It says: when you're a god,
you got responsibilities to your constituents.   Or
   some eggs may hatch but kitchens are for omelets or
if you can't take the heat don't lay an egg.
Thus the GREAT EQUALIZER decrees that some be tranquilized
and others freneticized, that there be generals and hoplites,
winners and losers, Caesars (1 each) and slaves
And keepers (of course) and kept.
   Now it is a matter of imperial indifference whether you and
I, cits, dimwits, midges, near zeroes, non heroes, whether we
exist or no. But one thing is clear; in our regard the myth of
Genesis has been turned around. Henceforth to read:
   In the beginning was Skinner's labyrinth.
The furry humanoids, deloused, decorticated, lobotomized,
housed, fed, schooled by the state
   totally environmentalized   a synthesis of formally partial
structures (university, madhouse, prison, cinema, food trough,
sex bed, church) these scamperers and scavengers by dint of
expertise and electrode have learned
when to fear when to love when to piss when to feed when to
praise when to –
What one might miss in their makeup (were he a backward
looker, did he dare search for certain nearly submerged char-
acteristics of the tribe)
  is a certain
light in the eyes ('like shining from shook foil') a plumbless
interiority, a tease and come on, something funky in youth,
wrinkles as of laughter about aged brows, a sip in your eye look
of fire and ice
OR at the least a glimpse of Edens lost a look of scarce contained
grief, as for other shores horizons estuaries, 'blue remembered
hills',
yes – outraged love.

But no.

Bugged brainwashed buggered beggared besotted
Out of head and heart
or let us say, so nearly
out of head and heart
as to make no whit difference
to cast no grain of grit
in the armored almighty progress
of the warmongering worm
NO. SO.
HIS ALTITUDINOUS ARSITUDE, SPITTLE THE FIRST,
                              ANNOUNCES FROM THE
IMPERIAL BUNKER: THE ALTERNATIVES ARE HEREBY
                              EXPUNGED. KAPUT.

2.
Well almost.   Then again hardly.
Let us coolly, hardily
to fields away
make hay under the arc
that fans out, dawn
after hit and run dark.

3.
No to their NO.   Yes to all else.

4.
It is Christmas
the pride of peacocks
the birth of a child
his many forms
rising swaying around him
like eyes in feathers
dances harvests brides
resurrections
and underside
his shadowed

befallings
Pray; those eyes
touching our eyes
make us that man.

Con Cowan

The indefectible long reach,
The promise
That the mystery shall never be exhausted or polluted
Comes to rest – where?
I used to think, popes, lords, satraps,
Are the splendid repository, the stiff sleeve
From which issues the hand
Narrowing to a digital
That set free the milklike flood on Adam's bones
And the breath of the cosmos
Entering the blue rose
Lung of an infant
A polyp, a parachute of silk, dreamily
Launched for a landing . . .

Yes, no.   Now occurs to me
The face of Con Cowan, 17 years dying, less than a year
Resurrected.   By you, Fay and Bert
Conspiring with us, poor to the poor.
He was gray and bloodlet, stamped "bad meat"
By the butcher state.

Now
His eyes
dead fish
leap
quicksilver under the (God knows)
Modest bait of our recovery room – laughter, decency, above all
That promise, simple as bread in our hands
The hands of friends
Hustling him breathless out
Of the death house
Into the free form dance
We improvise day after day
And shall never (promise)
Die in the doing.

December 2, 1971

One of them, a benign corrupt cop
with the face of a bishop's crook
locks me in, jocund at midnight.

Goose pimples, recognition
an Auschwitz moment
as if a renegade jew
ushered his rabbi, with a flourish, a persuasive
push
into
"our best yes sir absolutely Grade A reserved oven."

For Philip's Birthday

1.
Praise God I say yes
Even for deprivations!
Starved in nostril and eye
we make do, make do
With near stocks and stones,
Flat approximations
of the squamous and famous real things
Which if I could I would
Make come true for you
Like godmother or god.

But knowing how justice burns
In a brother's fingertips
Knowing nothing is won
Neither will, passion, sustenance,
Freedom or freedom's outreach
Until all, all are fed –
And standing somewhat this side
Of almighty wheel and deal –
What can I make for you?
Simulacra, images,
cosmic complicity
with all that lives and moves
On earth's majestical
Land mass and waterfall.

2.
Remembering why we are here, remembering
As we down the pinchbeck food, as we drown our sighs
At the gut-deranging absurdity, being here.
Remembering, refusing the flabby amnesia
Of rule, rote and rot; remembering.
Doing time; time hard or easy,
No matter, with outreach

And gut, swallowing small troubles, trips.
Doing time, mark it.   The following miss the mark;
False heads, flatulent gods.

No; doing it all, giving all, giving the lie
To the briefcased hardbacked softpates
Whose *yes* is a no no.
Doing time,
Not clockwise
But counter with anger,
countering
The rickety deceits, the cracked dome above, the sky
a runnel –
Rotten consensual juices.

3.
Because we remember, it is possible to dismember
The demon haunted will.   Why we are here.
A thighbone
Wreathed with its laurel flesh, walks on and on
Toward the promise.
Because we remember our Father
It is possible to be sons.   Because we remember
Our brothers, it is possible
To bind up wounds we never dealt.
Possible.
Unbungled, courageous, birth and 2nd birth
on and on – new phases,
Genetic transfigurations.
The thighbone
One, alive, remembering, incandescent, soul.   Toward.

4.
The reason we are in prison encompasses
The harmonies of nature; visible, invisible, beneficent.
To bring these connections home

Plunging one's wrists
Into the sources and springs of being
So cold they scald,
Lifting eyes to the dispassionate heavens
So distant they blind.
We wear like a flower our reason; it endures.
We compose our reason, a prayer; God bends to it.
O place us in the very tic and mortal danger
Of self renewing choice, the heart riding its high wire!
We are here neatly as crystals telling time.
A nest of woven thorns, swans' down,
haven of the warm unborn,
desert and arctic temperatures; survival.
More; the grace that renders gracious.
O delighting Spirit, we are here; grant space.

5.
In a bad time good religion?   Rare, so rare,
Like wild strawberries or thyme in factory
Slag, hardly ever.
Wherever growth; rank, outrageous.

Jesus freaks, born with a 3rd throttling
Hand, contemplators drowned like drunken
Sailors in the sap of their navel, actionists
bloodying the ape in the mirror
That beats them bloody, a bloody bore.
Religion?   At the edges it were better to keep silence.

6.
What finally to hope for?   something enduring
might come of simple endurance, a cheerful mien,
sight of moon and stars, faces
that mirror across the void, our faces.
Harsh, hardly victory.
The logical text of the years leads to this place.

Make then, like a Greek ecstatic, virtue of necessity.

7.
With us it was never
winner and loser
but you, a big AND,
and I and our two hands.
Who cared if overhead
napkined and beaked
in the air a buzzard stink
in the air the wrong gods!
heel to heel, we ran.
Both
made it, death to life.
So no hindmost and no
devil to take either.

8.
Those eyes, icy and fiery at once
a sky lashed by an equinoctial sea
a way of reminding:
   Don't confuse brute turmoil with human change!
Pointing to the confusion did not end it, granted.
He drew a line, a horizon,
   the sea's fury
withdrew; sea and sky, demure as a new bride and groom in
                                                    public.
   You had to imagine their act of love, could not.
We turned away murmuring, mystery
      gazing, bathing
      drowned, eluded,
"the friend of the bridegroom, rejoicing."

My Father

1.
All bets were on; he was dying
back in '62; found by mother 2:00 a.m.
on the john floor, bleeding end to end mightily.
Toward dawn I was summoned;
A jungle of tubes and bowls; going out big,
the symbols of mortician culture
blooming around like fungi.
He lay there weak as childhood.
They were filling him, an old sack,
with new wine.   He took it darkly.
"When the wheat's ready for harvest,
draw it in," all I remember.
Strong enough behind his milky cat's eyes
to spin a trope about death, strong enough to live.
Foul January dawn
beetled down upon us, he lay there like a switchblade
awaiting the spring, awaiting death
like a palmed blade.   No takers . . .

2.
Phil goes in chains to Harrisburg today
I sit here in the prison ward
nervously dickering with my ulcer
a half-tamed animal
raising hell in its living space.
Time to think once more of my father.
There were photos, brown, detailed
tintypes.   You had only to look
(30, 40, years ago)
for the handsomest bucko present.
It was uncanny.
A head of burnished locks, a high brow
a cynic's sidelong look.
Boyo!   You kept at center eye
the eye of storms.

In a mad Irish way "all there." Whole apple, one bite.
The mouth reminds me of a whip;
sensual and punishing.
Tasting the world, sexually alive,
calling the tune, paying the piper.
He was chaste as an Irish corpse,
Mother-maidensister-haunted.
We 6 were as much emblems of expiation
as of seasonal bedding
each of us sponsored by the church
like a first class relic or a nun's goody.

3.
I wonder tonight in Danbury Prison
in the damned off-season of human beings
an ulcer kicking at my groin
like the sour embryo of Nixon's next brainchild
I wonder –
the Jesuits staring 'round like frogs of the Nile
at baby Moses –
I wonder if I ever loved him
if he ever loved us
if he ever loved me;
an undersized myopic tacker
number 5 in pecking order
pious maybe, intelligent I guess
looking for corners where half in, half out
he could take soundings,
survive, emerge; protective coloration.
Not enamored of the facts of life
i.e., sledgehammers, chicken little,
the cracking muscles of the strong.
As a child you expect violence; the main issue
somehow to clear away
space and time
to survive in.   Outside the circle, who cares?

DANIEL BERRIGAN   48

He exacted performance, promptitude,
deference to his moods
the family escutcheon stained with no shit.
The game was skillful (we never saw it so well played
elsewhere), he was commonly considered
the epitome of a just man.
We sat on our perches blinking like six marmosets.
There were scenes worthy of Conrad;
the decks shuddering;
the world coming to end!

He is dead now.
The conduct of sons and priests
is not grist for news-hawks and kites.
When my mother (who surely
suffered most at his hands) read one account
served up by an esteemed scribe
she wept for shame and loss.
There is more honor, more
noblesse oblige, more
friendship with reality, more unconscious graceful wisdom
in the least gesture of her
little finger, than in
the droppings and screams of the whole preening profession
of whooping cranes.
The office of charity, of classic
Pietàs, fills the vacuum
around that absent figure
with the presence of compassion.   My father –
when in '39 I braced and dug in
for the great leap, I was one
of 38 candidates for priesthood.
All excelled me
in arts, language, math,
self-assurance, the golden number of
the Jesuit dance.   32 years later

I sit in Danbury Prison for illegal
acts contrary to war.
Father
I close my eyes, conjure up
like a deaf-mute mimic
your ironic ghost.   How convey
my gratitude, my sense
of the delicious rightness of things?
Whatever you denied us, you
gave us this, which enemies name
distemper, madness; our friends,
half in despair, arrogance.
Which I name, denying both – the best of
your juice and brawn, unified
tension to good purpose.
Prosit, requiescat.
The bad news drones on
plague after seventh plague
hypnotic, futile as an argument
for God's existence

4.
Sat by the tube at 7 p.m.
longing for salvation.   None.
Etsi Deus non daretur.   What if
faith like a talisman flew
above the reeking decks where
my friends died, mad of thirst,
one by one?   would there be faith?
I last held a child in my arms, courtesy
of the Federal System of Prisons
on Thursday, April 2, '71, around 2:00 p.m.;
an adopted 5 year old, Carla,
my niece.   She ran to my arms
across the gray visitors' room, unconscious
of my felonious garb, the washed out military

khakis, several sizes big,
incongruous as a general's playsuit
on a scarecrow.   No matter.   She loves
like a Trojan child, fiercely.
Her minute body is ambrosial,
her eyes are blue, and summon flowers
as desert springs do.   O this official
staked out desert, we make do
month upon month
sans flowers, children,
sea, horizons, wander like the weak dead
a few paces from appointed graves.
We need (A.J. Muste in old age)
a foreign policy for the children.
Present arrangements fall short
let us admit
of that modest attainable goal.
The guns of Calley calibrated,
focused
by less visible powers, the pitiful débris
of rag dolls, mothers, blood, mud –

tonight, April 3, the President
sickened our hearts toward death
once more, once more, the sore-mouthed clichés
of "national honor" whipped onstage –
the eve of Maundy Thursday!   Tomorrow
we prisoners break stale bread, our lives
broken like bones, the wheel of consciousness
hectoring us round and round and round the compound.
Caught in its spoke a flower, up from the
filthy late snow, eccolo!   Count 3 windows
north of the Inmates' Mess Hall, look downward
to ground level; a fallen bird, its haphazard
bones.   I have lived long, I have seen
many sorrows, a few moments vindicate

everything.   A man went seeking his love
in hell . . .

5.
The poem concerns children.   I came into sunlight
Maundy Thursday, reporting for work detail.
Snow past midnight, warming air.
On an old bench, an old rabbi
prison clothing, prayerbook, yarmulke
murmur of prayer.   *Your name,* he asked?
Berrigan.   Oh then you are Jewish?
Only, father, in expectation . . .
The poem, like the season, like the rabbi
like the blank-faced hacks, like the director of federal prisons
like My Lai, concerns children.
My father, asked what crop he grew
on the old farm outside Syracuse (depression
sour clay and drought); laconically:
boys!   One year, an old mare dragging a harrow
through the sparse corn rows, with the perfect timing
of senescence
reached a drain ditch
near the roadside, stepped down daintily
as a duchess, lowered her backside,
lowered her long face to her knees (harness
jangling like rude jewelry) lay there
saying from her eyes; next move, yours.
Tonight under a paschal moon, I mimed
a Goya etching in the
prison yard
3 shadows coming, growing
came, grew, vanished like footpads –
Jesus, Satan, that interdicting
third, weaving, bargaining, up to his ears
in bloody Friday; Lord, is it I?
Under the shrewd exhalation of the moon,

I bundle up to throat;   no
horse thieves, poachers,
informers in our blood!   Nicked by his razor, Dado
mutters in the mirror; *the blood of Irish kings!*
Mother at the stove, turns up her eyes to heaven . . .

6.
Letter from a commune;
the country is real
pretty now, spring thaw.   We have 4
white chickens, they lay an egg each day
occasionally minus a shell
Naomi our collie by some miracle
is not knocked up.   She got out
in torrid heat and 5
(no shit, 5) dogs awaiting her début
chased her into the woods.   She came back
hours later, tired and confused.
I'm building a weaving loom for Susan.
She just made herself a turkish sandwich.
But before she could get back to the table
Horace ate it!   Those animals
rip us off blind
and we look the other way . . .

7.
Dado's classical bent
left none unstigmatized.   A white billy-goat
was marvelously misnamed, to fanfare
from the dog, faint horselaugh from the mare;
Ursus.   He knocked the postman for a loop,
scattered mad Mamie Powell, chewed up,
in the side yard, until chased by sticks,
the shirt the '29 depression spared.
Crimes multiplying, stink
offending, he was sold off, reversing

the Judas trick, to metamorphose in paschal stew
in Little Italy, down country.   We mourned him –
hooves, pride of blood, horns of
neighborhood dilemmas, nattering mouth, pirate's eye,
the uncouth unreconstructed thieving
alter ego of six boys.

1930; Dado decreed a mercy death.
A splay-legged spavined nag
bit the dust, under an orchard tree,
Tom firing point blank.   Laziness
our virtue in common; we dug a shallow grave
heaped the cadaver over, like a
prairie cenotaph.   One week later, mother,
stringing the laundry from tree to tree
was shaken to tears and flight.   A colossal
long drawn fart issuing from the grave,
a strange unnatural
convulsion; earth heaved, ground opened,
a great equine rear leg shot up skyward.
The resurrection of the dead?
Weeks passed, sweet seasonal process
grounded the upstart sign, grounded my father's
Jovian lightnings . . .

8.
      In the old fables
   jays   macaws   jackals
 cowardly   inching forward   careening   hobbling   jeering
   surrounded the mysterious firebird.
   The figure and form of the age.
Philip; the little blond boy with lowered eyes
   in a blue fluted sweater
      stands to the left of me in a faded kodak film, 1927.
   You threw stones like a demon
   hid your windup locomotive in the old grey immigrant trunk.

In one year your limbs telescoped out
    a poet's brow, those commanding utterly blue eyes
a sapphire intensity, precision instruments taking
        the world's size.

    I do not know when the wager was first struck
I see another photo, a windy June day
    outside Washington Shrine, the family smiling,
a single-minded triumph; its ordained priest!
    war years, depression years   decently buried in albums
then that "stampede into religion"
        (John's sneering phrase)
    the church's chased cup
continuity, rounded latinate
    breaking up   breaking up

Dado,
your sons
close kept in Danbury Jail
keep Maundy Thursday.
You lie close too
after the 90 year uphill climb.
Pompey graveyard, a "sylvan close"
(your phrase) of trees and mounds
slopes westward, gentle, sunny.
Are you proud of your 2 priests
plucked by the sovereign state, for crimes
against war crimes?   The children of My Lai
like Fra Angelico's angels, make sport of death;
with instruments of harmony
keep green, for us, your grave.
Children – those natural buds
those nodes of process, rose red, snow white
first fruits of blood and semen, fallen rosy and white
to the spread aprons of women, fruits
of energetic love.   Who strikes them –

9.
In Catonsville Court,
evidence was taken; why did you burn
the government files?   (Ideologies
break like rot under the judge's hammer;   conscience an airy
game, unless its reach
touch like a ministering hand, the afflicted
flesh of the living.)
I looked to right and left
for symbols, realities.   To left, a flag.
To right, the jury's intent burdened faces.
I did not want the flag trailing the world
stained with blood
nor did I want the children and grandchildren
of the jurors to perish by fire.
The judge flushed to his ears.   *It is insupportable*
to claim a motivation six months after
events.   How could you have known, in May,
October's jurors or the jurors' children?
Silence.   I spread my hands.

10.
   Winters we chugged two miles to Sunday Mass
in a model-T snowbucker, old the year
   it was born.   Like a sailing fish it sported
flapping gills of isinglass and canvas.
   We bedded down like Peter Rabbit's litter, crowded
in the hold, eyes, cold noses, Dado
   pumping and worrying us along.   Spread over all
6 boys, a 7 foot square Buffalo robe
   gamey, coarse as porcupine.   Arrived, dismounted
at St. John Baptist
   we made an obedient huddle, awaiting
disposition of the steed.   The robe, pulled from the rear seat,
   made a splendid radiator noseguard
against deep freeze.

We sat at the children's Mass
singing from 5c notebooks the hymns
    we murdered all week to Sister's beating stick
Mother dearest Mother fairest; to Jesus' heart all burning.
    Monsignor McEvoy, our ample prophet, out of his
workday overalls (teacher, lawyer, builder)
    splendid as an iconostasis, humble as Nazareth
gave us a children's gospel.   Not bad; religion
    stuck to our Sunday bones . . .
If we went mad, it was
for sweet reason's sake;
to wish all children well; to make of the world's breakup
cup, loaf, murder, horror, a first (or last) communion.

    Aunts Aggie, Maggie, Elizabeth, Mollie, Bird the nun,
Uncle Johnny, Ned the priest, Dado,
    held Sunday pow-wow in the family long house
on Matson Avenue.   Mother, born German
    never quite made the caucus.   Al Smith, Father Coughlin
were house penates.   Once a year
    New Year's Day, Mom and "the gang"
(Maggie's put-down) were summoned
    to state dinner.   I remember
straight chairs, straight talk, kids
    frozen to our seats by the old maids'
steely looks; indifferent food, Maggie
    dispensing into shirt pockets, on the hour
with a teaspoon, her stony pacifier, "Loft's Hard Candies."
    They were straight out of Port Royal, Maynooth,
Oneida, pure as angels, proud as devils.
    My father's marriage stuck in the throat of virtue.
Upchuck or swallow; the discreet dilemma
    was audible for years, burp, cover up.

Grandmother Berrigan's portrait
    looked down in mild wonderment,

a queen above a nest of bickering kites
   she, troubled, questioning
the trick and treat of time's outcome – 11 children, a widow
on Christmas day
   of '74.   Grandfather, bleeding
from immigrant's lung,
   A daughter ran outside
to break the ice on the rain barrel, plunge a chunk
   into his mouth.   His body hauled
up scoured December hills in a democrat wagon
   to lie where my father would lie.
Dado slept that day, a child
   in a farm woman neighbor's arms . . .
I set this down
   in Danbury Jail; Philip and I
priests, first (for all we know) to break
   trust of the clan, trust
again and again, like Jansenius'
   first rule of order; first pass-fail;
no one, not one of the
   family, ever in jail.

11.
In old Assumption church on Salina Street
a phony dungeon on the dark rear stair
kept con Jesus under lock.
We crept down
during the long noon hour,
Lucifugae, sprats, beguiled
by darkness and vigil lights, prayed there
some better outcome for the man, caught in the twin
pincers of church and state.   Would Pilate
dash the bowl to ground, would Caiaphas convert? . . .
Holy Saturday I set this down
by courtesy of the twin powers, doing time.
Jesus, lift head tonight from the foul grime

of churches.   Thorns like bees
drone at the skull; does sacrifice bring in
straight on a beeline, honey, money, honor?
The dull eyes focus under a full moon
outside my window, resplendent
to frame a face in the informer's kiss.   Who knows?   Who
                                                    knows?

a bargain struck
in silver, brings it down; rain, ruin
piece by piece, indictments on the 6
Harrisburg peacemakers, Berrigan et al
versus United States . . .
My grandmother's head
turns side to side, dubious as a ghost.
We teased mother.
Tom, Tom, the farmer's son,
why did you ever marry that one? –
(she blushed)
Indeed?   He was considered quite a catch!

12.
November dawn, 1969, your jaw dropped, a semaphore
        the last train out of ghost town.
We gathered in 2 brown sacks
        everything you owned, an immigrant pauper's bundle

I leaned over the bed, breathing for you
        all that night long
        (somebody else was there)
        2 shadows over a fish tank
        helpless as men watching the death
        of the fish from whom
        all men, fathers and sons, ad infinitum, come

A fish metamorphosing
        into a father before our eyes –

hands, feet, blue as a fish

I could not take you in my arms, give you back
        wits, volatile energy
        confounding moods, appetite
        the farm, drought, depression years
        the scythe that whistled
        like a wood plane across hard earth

Did you want it all back anyway?
        Think.   6 sons, 5, 4, 3, 2, 1, –
        then nothing, a wedding night, a bride
        life awaiting doing all again?

You hated like hell that necessity
        we lived by – your scant love
        the stigma
        it took years to heal; making do,
        fear, damnation, fury.

Well we made it; some deep root of sanity
        we sucked on.   Above,
        the idiot thrashing storms you made

Maybe it was your face dropping its mask
        asleep over a book,
        Irish intelligence; now and again
        a piercing stab of virtue; a boy
        kneeling beside you at Mass; a 6 yr. old
        rocking-horse Catholic.

Thank you old bones, old pirate
        old mocker and weeper.
Could have lived to a hundred.   But contrary passion
set in hard; falling downstairs
that last time, into your own

unconscious.   To hell with it; bag it all.
a bloody act of the will, a fever nursed by rage.   Sons
no longer mitigating presences, who
now and again had been;
        has been now.   You turned to the wall.

And I have no recourse except
hatred and love, your hand
breaking through earth
nightmare or miracle;
your face
muffled in its shroud
a falcon
disdaining
the dishonor nailing
us here
like stinking fish
(ancestors, sons)
to the world's botched cross

Landed, boned, buried in Pompey yard . . .
To see the performance, was scarcely
to believe it.   One summer night
he tipped
the kitchen table, set for supper, up on end
for some supposed infraction. He fought sons
to a sullen draw, told enchanting children's stories
of summer nights, wrote poetry
like a flaring Turk, absurd, byronic,
battled the land to a dust storm,
prayed, slept stertorously in the big
leather rocker, ate like a demon,
exacted instant "yes sir!   no sir!"
died like a sword swallower choked on
his breath's long blade . . .
The old house breathed relief

in his absence.   None of us could, those years,
were screws turned on our thumbs, confess
to love him.
Was it that dearth of love
turned us to the long tragic way
on and on?   What measure
of that irascible spirit, lodged unappeased
in us, bears, endures, survives – even
Danbury?   One virtue awaits
the arresting fist of death.
Until: Walk on, Take breath, Make do.

In blinding Minnesota winter sun
one of the older brothers
would hoist a kid up, pick-a-back, and run.
I was 3 or 4; John trundled me round the yard
ducked suddenly into a dark wood shed
striking me blind.   Against my face
some rough pelted thing swayed frozen.
Recovering sight
screamed, screamed like a banshee, a child
gone mad for terror;
a frozen timber wolf's death-head
hung by a thong from the rafters, eyes open
bloody mouth –

   The stuff of nightmares or of dental chairs.
   In Danbury Clinic
I urge the wary inmates; *open wide now;*
a superannuated paraclete, all in white
for the liturgy; needles and drills
   needles and drills.   Domestic policy, we juice
America's pain to sleep.

   The reason I am juicing
pain to sleep your honor: deep in the jaws of hell

the cries of children throb.   A demon, a judge
would win (I judge) respite for whatever
    mortal offense had sunk him down
could he
    turning from pain of loss,
hear on the firestorm, near, endearing
    as a flute note, a reveille in hell,
the cry of a child.   Could he
    weep for the death of children,
possibly would mount, stage on stage of Hell
    by transfer order, Springfield to Atlanta
to Lewisburg – to the first circle
    Danbury!

    Daily, the high-class haloed crooks
open their jaws like hippos or the church,
    ascend in the pneumatic chair, float there
in horizontal beatitude.
    Trinitarian light
pours down.
    Teeth or doubloons?   Bridgework,
gorges, an intricate A.A. map
    of paradise.   We stand aside; the meritocracy
makes mock of tinkers.

In thè wink of an eye, graves shall open
the dead arise.   Easter morning
I write: dearest mother, many friends
bring flowers to your bedside, smiles
from Danbury.   We are well, our thoughts
are thanks.   Thanks to you, the instrument
of truth, who plucked us by the hair
harebrain and all, from false peace.   Alleluia.

What Is the Opposite of Charisma?
Dedicated to Mr. K., in the Kafkian Sense

Life is what it is, a matter of
lowest common survival.   Dry, sexless, a
walking shambles, Ichabod Crane's
protoplast;
threat under bribe under
pietism; a liturgical feast of
inanities.   He plucks like Chuzzlewit
the rotten catgut that sets his religious
bowel throbbing: "Dan, some of us
are Catholic.   Do you know
the vast respect in which we hold you?"
Refuses us the courtesy
of shared vitriol.   Yet his silly putty face
shakes like a porridge into spurious life
as the avenging angel hovers.   Deep seated
hatred, spite, "pure intention."
We have shaken from sleep
the first of 7 inhabiting devils.
O Mr. K., Catholic, egoist, liberal
in the ancestral sense that cut down
Socrates in mid-sentence: "There are those
who make the worse the better argument."
There; it always ends in murder.
It was the circumcised, the brothers
of a single convenant, cried out
in blood lust: His blood be on us.

Mr. K., I am told, is father
of 2 fair sons.   I have not seen them.
I have seen their father, I fear
for the sons.   I fear for the sons of
every father who issues forth at morning
invulnerable to burning arrows
that make of him, were he clothed
in human tegument, one chorus of

DANIEL BERRIGAN   64

voluble tongues, wounds, a Saint
Sebastian before the furies.
I fear, justly or not, for the sons.
My argument: Mr. K. loving them
the more, in pride of station, easing
them, himself, Mrs. K., their growing
rightful share of goods and chattels –
up, up the tilted ladder to Olympus,
never thinks, for solicitude
of their well-being, their most tender
plaint or whim, their sweet
ignorance, inquiry, outbreak of joy –
never thinks . . . whose flesh,
pays the excursion fare, whose bodies
bound, gagged, confined in place
like wood rungs in sockets
make possible this almost in-
-corporeal ascension, this success story,
the stormers of heavenly places,
the necromancers of eternity
whose pure breath turns crude shekels
to crystal lozenges, for purchase
of loge seats before the IMMACULATE LAMB . . .

It would be manifestly unjust
(justice presupposing consciously
executed choice, e.g., my sweet flesh
before yours)
to assign like an obscene placard
stuck covertly to a virtuous
tweed back, guilt to Mr. K.
To wit: you are, in your modest local scope
a criminal of note.

Nevertheless.
Item: before noon

on given weekdays, you (Mr. K.) increase
by perceptible degree, the intensity
of active misery in prisoners' eyes.

Item: where you cannot kill (that being,
in the generals' method of immediate
let blood, verboten) you sow confusion; the technician's
strategy, come to the same end.

Item: you lead prisoners
by the hand, a solicitous mad baptizer
into the polluted stream of Esalen, Skinner,
Behaviorism, "Psychology Today" —
immerse them, in the name
of Insensitivity, Sterility and
Obfuscation.   In Whose invocation
the prisoner, held under,
fixed, transfixed, clotted, clogged,
is invariably
dragged out, dead as haddock.
Which is to say, signed with the stigma
of Beast, Burden and Bunkum.
He can now prate, to no point or
outcome, of "my reaction to you,
yours to me."   Me fa so la.
The feet thump, the player piano
makes like Chopin.   Holiday
in the wax-works.

Item: in your pious hotfoot circle of
foxes and geese, you always win.
Always drag someone, by the bird-brain, home
for dinner.   In other circles
this is named the circular argument:
we had (sadly) *to destroy them*
to save them.   History

assigns these words, by wit of implication
to the shadowy operator, J. Iscariot.

O Mr. K!
would have us affectionate
toward authority.   Likes us
earnestly.   Is more dangerous
than any redneck, his weapon
the decadent last ditch strength
of rotten intellect.   His tongue
flares like a consumptive's brow.
Ascribe to him 20 perfectly
unflapped arguments – how
in the Better Business Bureau where
mickmocks make their mockups
the prison factory's buzzer
like Roland's classic horn
trumpets: *human betterment!   betterment!*

20 years ago, a prison built for
450.   Today, 750 to 800 inmates.
Then, a large
percentage of inmates worked the fields,
raked, hoed, harvested, lazed
summers long, long-limbed Connecticut hills.
This was judged essentially unproductive.
Connecticut was earthquaking
like the armory of Mars; General
Dynamic, submarines, copters.
A prison functionary, struck
with epidemic lightning, created
like fire in dry straw
the future on the instant.
They sold the farm to hippies, the prisoners
to the war god.   Today the inmates slouch,
sound of the horn, to factories; cable

assemblies for missiles.   Thus
the perfect corporate circle is closed;
the poor, Blacks and Spanish, for
slave wages, fashion eradicators
of their opposite numbers: the poor of southeast
Asia.   To kill off your intractable
kinsmen, profitably to yourself
thus reducing world pressure on the
lid that all but lifts off the
iron pot, rattling and booming like
makeshift musketry –
"Change of methods, change of masters" –

Chestnuts, glowing coals, raked
from the fire.   The fire cools, the pot
tempers and seals.   A ritual
of regret; too bad, a few, so to speak,
burned fingers.
"Things prisonwise" (the abominable
coinage is his own)
"have improved, improvement will continue."
He nods like a king's metronome.

What king?   What bloody
regent in one of history's grander
peaks, a degenerate Constantine,
killer and Christian, X'd out
for Xt's sake, the last intractable
stain of redskin rage?   Correct.
Who made of black skins a sad sack wherein
broken bones might shuffle about
breathing "yassuh" at a Massah's breathing
arse?   Correct.   Who seized on the mealy-mouthed
religiosity of Quakers, offered
malefactors a 2-pronged "option";
1.) time, time, good time, hard time

segregated, the unnatural sons
of that prolix madam Res Publica; and
2.) A BIBLE, the dualistic rot
lent a divine coherence: God's localized
damnation, sober warning to
clucking burghers, sucking virgins,
tomcat children.   Who?   Correct.

Appalled, I think of the children.
Gotten by fathers whose veins throb
for the world's jugular.

"My love!" –
A hand reaches in hot excess of love
to quench the light, to quench
the light of the world.   Into a naked
lovelit body, releases
hot weaponry, liquid
firefall.   On distant
sleeping children, not one's own.
Not our own!
The eyes, the loose flung limbs,
the pâpier maché faces,
the ashes sown to the bitter winds –
O Mr. K!

When My Brothers Fasted For Me

June 1971

1.
When my brothers fasted for me,
they fleshed out the skin of survival
they fleshed out the soul, thinning themselves
in that desert carnival
where the devil rides Quixote
like an ass the spine of a man

and three temptations stalk; (1) all is bread
to the capital gain of the brain, and
(2) throwing your weight around gives
employment to idling angels, and
(3) where the devil pisses perfume, let
God bend his knee.

2.
If I were the last
felon in lockup, my brothers
would fast for me.
(The statement
ignores
a bloodshot fact: man
is a cage constructing animal.)
Fasting for a brother thus becomes
in the curious Marxist phrase, a "class action."
Self-denial releases, like a pierced heart
enormous consequence.
As though man the cagemaker –
whose hand like a bloody stump
must be fitted to a lethal claw
key
gun
to "feel right" with the anthropology of manifest destiny –
were grabbed by an epiphany from the clouds of heaven
and dropped those deadly prostheses,

(flexing his ten fingers
flexing his forked being
into a peace sign)
or stranger still,
wept from his bull's eye eyes.

3.
Denying the good things of the world thus becomes
good news for the world.   Bread refused
goes further.
The bread tree of the universe
savors in its sap, the blood and sweat
that fell to its soil, a laborer's bloody sweat.
Those speaking leaves
bestir; *stand*
at beginnings!

4.
So much hogwash, the "spiritualized universe"
that had never been
carnal;
conflated with the divine
that had never twisted in knots
for a violated brother.
Hypocrite renunciation!
the rose shall impale the eyeball,
the grape gripe
like a serpent's toil
that groin, that hedonist gain!

on the birth of dan goldman: a song of triumph

my 50th year having arrived
and striding so to speak the heights –
i.e., recently appointed
Laureate In Residence At The Imperial Madhouse,
Woebegone Acres.   Duties: the striking
of dawn and twilight fires, incantations
communalities, observances,
a spartan rigor, open air,
 work, study, prescience of stern eyes

well   on a certain dawn like any
other dawn   (dawn here being dusk
inside out;   the whole
backward   forward
a single fabric
woven by mad   fingers   under which
freudian legerdemain makes
bad miracles   remorse   sour tears)

a birth!
in this landlocked hell   a dove bore
in his beak   a missive
scrawled in a day-old hand
dropped   a flower at my feet
it cried   or the dove cried   or the child
I am born!   born!

and I could not believe it and
was thereby confirmed a man
whose birth his parents
for very joy   theirs their parents
and so on
could not believe

the closing of eyes
being much more our skill

than raising like a wineglass
the bloodied child for a blessing

I must tell (the telling
hurts like his mother's wound
his father's passion   compassion)
Jack, Beatrice, parents
I hear this little boy Dan
pipe like a lamb   *God is my judge*
one hand in his mother's   one
in his father's hand   he withstands
the mechanical bullies of the world
death   the undoer of children

Jailhouse   underground
the stinking alleys   fair Ithaca
the slave farms   fair Cornell
the poor languish   die by decree
those fields of combat
where cowards dread show face –

No, fields of joy!   a child's
metaphysical purity dawns
on the befouled world
parents   strangers   friends
Philip and you and I and
the cheated Asian children
first breath wrung from last
all   all are drawn, all
born, twice born, solve
resolve the mystical dance.

One Tries Hard to Mean These Words

Let us pray: forgive the big ones   Father
who pull down   capricious wreckers
your mild and serviceable earth.
See deep   perplex long above
the plumbless pit of their wrongdoing
who devise   triumphant   cast in face
of you and yours   their tricky and tinny wares
dare fashion yes   to your thunderstruck gaze
idols   foul proximates
through clacking jaws to mime   mock you

Nevertheless forgive them Father straightway   hard and fast
bind up voracious wounds   for surgeon appoint
the meek of the earth   their hands
acquainted   as yours   with wounds   empty
of base-won gain.   Groans of the sinner
groans of the healer   resound in you
concomitant   a second birth.
Bear us a new heart   Majesty   save
all things your tears and mirth called forth

Prisoners: One Only View

In the dark movie house
they curse and scream like tartars. Come back
2, 3 times, to snatch
like sticky children,
bobbing big balloons
that wear
smaller balloons in privy places.
They steal food like raping crows.
They steal clothing.   They steal
like lice on carrion, blood.
They do not honor the Lord thy God on Sunday
beseemingly.   No; snore, fart, turn like stoats
on a picnic spit,
believe in eye-for-an-eye-for-an-eye, would strike
if could, world blind as a crater.

Prison: A Place Where Death Didn't Quite Make It

So much death, death in official skulls!
Then
joyous talents, evocation of young minds,
everything we have striven for.   That men draw together
denying in that fervor, the prevenient yawn of death.
So much life!   we sprawl on the parched grasses
around a guitar, plaintive.   A captive hand
releases strings.

So much life!
we have made of this place of death a burial ground
a potter's field.
Death drawn, quartered
cut down, limed, a beast's bone
tossed to the wolves of time.
They howl sometimes, but are quiet now.
And we stand, men on men's shoulders
and see.   And death
like a carrion
lies

No One Knows Whether Death, Which Men in Their Fear Call the Greatest Evil, May Not Be the Greatest Good

It may be expedient to lose everything.
The moon says it, waxing in silence, the fruit of the heavens,
     grape vine, melon vine.
    Autumn upon us, the exemplar, the time of falling.
  One who has lost all is ready to be born into all:
    buddha moon   socratic moon   jesus moon
      light and planet and fruit of all:
"unless the grain falling to earth die, itself remains alone"

The Day the Humming Birds Returned, and Why

You should see us sweating out St. Matthew's Gospel
like 3 hunched safecrackers, bending
felonious skills to the black box, the book,
like a brass banded
chastity belt whose formula
father keeps locked even from
the pearl-diver's daughter.   Astonishing!
We sweat and stew: a break-and-entry man,
a safecracking high scorer, yours truly.
Astounded, finding our opposite no.'s
grinning back from those pages,
through the chastened
second thoughts of the twice born.
Losers, con men, pimps, felons, healed by the astringent
application to afflicted parts of severally –
(1) No shrinks, hollowing
our gourds into spittoons for the rabid effluence
of suppurating smiles
(2) No lying high wide and handsome bribes
of transfer from birdshit acres to dog-ditto.
(3) No Barbie Doll preachers
the word locked in mid-crotch
or more precisely *in casu*
blind in no man's land.

The Earth

When earth yielded up to our arms
the multitudinous children of her invention –
streams, starlight, storms – we were the pampered lovers then
of those who loved us, one flesh and blood, one bone.
O that embrace the state's steel gauntlet
raced down on like a wild fire.   Wounded
in nearest parts, part men only,
we wind, unwind our bloodied limbs,
feverish, icy, swept by what sighs and tides . . .

Skunk

The only fauna admitted
to the widespread country zoo
(every animal in his natural
habitat, no visible bars)
was an unloquacious
bumbling skunk.
He crept in under the full moon
like a moon thing, eyes
dazed, moonstruck.   Limped
along unhandily, as though
on 5 feet or 3, footsore.
Looking for what?
We wished
he would breathe deep
as an ancestor, metamorphose
10 times his size
piss high as a Versailles fountain
his remarkable musk perfume.
We didn't want additional
prisoners, even dumb ones.
If they must come, atavistic,
mystical, then let them be
spectaculars, trouble-
shooters.   O skunk, raise
against lawnorder, your grandiose
geysering stinking *NO!*

A Bit of History

Those Jesuit fathers (wrote Isaac Jogues from New France)
who purpose volunteering for these wilds
    and the service of their Indian brothers
        had best leave behind all regret for
university degrees, honors, prerequisites.
The questions raised by their clients will be other
    than the subtleties their minds
      sharpened and shone on, elsewhere.
TO WIT: can they bear heartbreaking portages
    survive on sour pemican
live under intense extremes of heat, cold, solitude?
The times mitigate the questions, never quite stilling them.
    As I learn, my middle cast cranium
      bending to the intricacies, simplicities
              of a new a b c.

Flowers in Spite of All

Truth; the long alas   alas uttered
in this charnel house at every hour.
                                    Then
the luxuriant splendor of flowers
in the prison beds
                    (ungenerous
unnourishing unfree impure air)
All the *via negativa*, the purgation
in which men wilt like spiritless blooms –
the flowers make heresy, make sport, give lie to!
they breathe like rising suns, they take no base measure
of man's blasted hopes, virulent fears.   Extraordinary
the reproving virtue of lowly tissues and emblems
renewing the earth, a saving remnant.

The day falls like a guillotine.
Man dies like Orpheus among flowers.

Memory

Killdeers that once like leaves in autumn tempests
flitted   hobgoblins around my evening walks
in the hills about Syracuse
     cry again in the prison yard.   My mind
is lit like a subterranean mine   like a trapped miner
that cry   that light
       as though salvation were at hand
(that cry   that light dimly seen)
          and the failing man
sighed   bitter in failing air
       too late   too late

We Were Poor Poor Poor

In prison remember
Dame Poverty, her strait uses of man;
Merton's photo, friend, confidant, brother under the skin
peering like young Picasso from the wall, a papery resurrection;
postcards, remnants
hung like the hanged from the cage wall.
Poverty: half your wits about you; the better half, a wife
gone off, a better offer.
O how fervently
we good burghers built jails, paid taxes for their upkeep.
Now they try us for size!
Brought down to size.   Procrustes broke us like cordwood.
"my tears   my tears   flow in the night"

Glory Be to God

we have not died on matterhorn no nor hearts popped like
                                                    bladders
    shot to the warm sea surface, pearl-diving.   Nor heads
                                                    blown off
by furious visionaries   nor in deserts perished far from springs.
   an unsteady hegira   an exodus   –   into what?
    gloria patri   we were forbidden to ask

Uncle Sam, You're a Card!

Whenever I meet a crook, newly arrived
(con man, forger, stocks and bonds)
I think gratefully
as we pump damp hands
of Uncle Sam.
Strangely also, of that dancing bear
who used to command
to heave himself up on slack legs
and flog about, an obscene pandemonium
like 5 men in a bear skin
up and down rue Madame
in Paris, in '64.
Every day the gypsies led him out
chained at the neck, in a different scrap of costume –
a gypsy, a drunk, a clown,
rags tossed on him that a.m.
from ashcans or the Paris dump.
1 and the same act, 1 moth eaten bear;
a cancer patient, a befuddled gypsy, a prisoner.
of terror or rage; eyes of a winded horse,
the fathomless liquid eyes, devoid
You could see, if you wished to see

under the mask, the battered stove pipe hat –
This is what makes of pity a useful virtue.

I pump hands with the latest middle-aged crook.
He played dominoes with Uncle Sam and lost.
Everyone loses.   Or rather, a sufficient number of suckers
to keep the game dangerous,
a public display of captive bears.
Each of them
dances here
9 months or a year, a chain
dangling from his neck (Lt. Strychnine
calling the shots)

clothed like an animal, from the U S dump.   Some call it
eating crow.

The crows laze overhead
like débris from the industry stack.
Day and night, for slave wages
the prisoners make war instruments
to drop on Vietnamese peasants.   This integrates
captive bears with the "national effort."
The local shrinks in gov't hire
urge the prisoners into the factories
with psychological cattle prods.
Early parole is the reward
for bears who dance
as though their foot pads smoked
on hot coals.

The diet is crow.
Some go mad on it.
A prisoner broke his chain
climbed the water tower
befuddled, trying to catch crow
on the wing.   Fellow-bears
gathered in knots below, bellowing
obscene encouragement: jump, you motherfucker!

Sometimes (rarely, once or twice)
pumping hands
with this or that crook, you see
flash out
not that old sodden lidded look of defeat
but the game, the click, the authentic old
killer himself –
the eyes of Uncle Sam.

This is what makes of anger a useful virtue.

200 years old, about to celebrate
the bicentenary of his revolution;
the look of a war poster.
Uncle Sam Wants You.

You're damn right he does.
The look goes through my body like a needle.
To wit –
This one is light on his feet.
The Russian bear is yesterday's cub
compared with this one.
Compared with this one, your kind
is practically extinct.

As to the future, any future.
you are advised to (China, Russia, you)
consult this one.

A Desert Painting I Saw in Here, Badly Reproduced

It is undoubtedly required
all one's life long
to plod about, useful
as a sourdough's mule, the prose
of one's flat feet, inmost
ruminations, matching
the splayed line
of an ass's back,
going
returning
(if lucky)
bowed like a shot bow,
under the hundredweights
of some el dorado.

Prose sometimes
yields to poetry
but only in the broken
jawbone of an ass
jawbone of a man

Friend, ghost
Georgia O'Keefe
put a desert
rose
in that bone dry urn
and walk on

The 3 Phases of Survival, As Follows

The spider that eyes you and me uxoriously
Making of marriage murder, or vice versa —
No.   I seek to assess the prison months of a blood
Brother, one half of whose full wine glass
I sip and pass to your hands;
As at the Mass
We make brotherhood of that mystic Third
Whose blood
Is mortise and mid-wife of memory.

The truth: they are trying to kill us.
Neither hyperbole nor obsession.   It is
First and last truth groaned by the turning locks.
Once we realize this — the steely
Self-willed purpose
Like leather and steel in a foaming mouth
Dragging the drover, making sport of
Hands frozen to reins —

We are in the third phase of common destiny.   Knowing this
We may once more put on, like wings or armor,
The imagery of our fate.   First phase: apparent autonomy
(Fair day, docile beast, morning red, evening gray)
Second phase: loss and more loss.
Third: compensation
A sublime exact arc of recovery
1 incident of which, as the beast slows, shivering to a halt
May well be one's own death.

Who says not?   This day, the watery eyed young medic
Set upon by a cloud of half mad inmates,
Assures me
He'd welcome another medical opinion on my case; but alas
The Prison Bureau thumbs down.   Also (smoothly) would I
                                        perhaps

Agree to surgery?
Prefer die (heat, gorge rising).
"So I thought" – dryly, point made, the politics of medicine
Traced out clear and bold
For astigmatics.   Sweat it out, kid
Or nerve failing, pluck it out.

Moonrise Over the Snow, Imagine!

After moonrise tonight the snow lay
like dust of age on green hair; even trolls age
under the moon, locusts, dragonflies, the green eyes
of bewitching sleeping girls, in old age.
Where foot fell, it was green on white
the peculiar uplifted purity of each on each.
As though prison salt were soil, grass a moon fire.
The lieutenant's foot from his dumb thigh, started fire.
And the warden's; where he witless and dauntless went.
And every defeated man shivered and shuffled
toward dead end, uncomforted.
Yet fire struck underfoot; a god,
or man, better.   He started and stole fire.

Fred

Cell next to mine dwells Fred, the *petit tailleur* of legend.
7 years jailed, 3 to go.   He fashions buddhas & crosses for free,
   shines shoes to an onyx mirror.
We are assailed night and day by cries
   of prisoners in solitary.   We sleep in snatches
the madames & pimps, their catbird calls, mockingbird calls
         exotic as an aviary.
Fred spits, polishes, minds his last.   Prison has bestowed on him
         air of decency, yea and nay speech of
peasants   farm helpers   bus drivers, those secret-faced men
whose big calliopes chug through the night.
   The thruway monks, I used to call them.

His cell is like the cab of a big truck; a trundle for sleep,
a few factory scraps.   Last week he fashioned for me
out of oddments a tiny model altar and sanctuary.
(tongue depressors, stick swabs, a towel rug)
   A campy triumph.   In that doll's church, a doll priest
cut down to size, might worship a god of prisoners
      kept too in a cage
like a rag picker's shack, a ragman's hope
   or the hope of a ragman God –
      the rank poverty of the universe.

Rehabilitative Report: We Can Still Laugh

In prison you put on your clothes
and take them off again.
You jam your food down
and shit it out again
You round the compound right
to left and right again.
The year grows irretrievably old
so does your hair burn white.
The mood; one volt above
one volt below survival,
roughly per specimen, space
sufficient for decent burial.

The Facts of Life Are, According to One Version, As Follows

American as the apple pie on your face,
include the common A. habit
of extending the carnivorous art
out, out, and out.
This specimen eats his way through the universe
eats
magic gems, lucky jars, spells of power, sovereign balms
wishing trees, cows of plenty, embodied beings.

It is not to be thought strange
if amid these aggrandized or diminished forms
(making up, so to speak, the solar system of appetite)
there should hang
on the universal yumyum tree
one or another conscious delectable morsel: you and me.

Now
to escape
the carnivores, dear terrified children, you must
propose to your flesh
a "radical alternative."
Can you be disjunctive, propose to others
a sublime YES, a choice made flesh, life made love?
so widen in the brute underbrush
chances of survival?
exuding in the direction of sundry powers the NO
of a humble will, a blood welcoming heart?

Memories Memories

In my ignorant salad days
(the middle 60's), the wife of the Sec. of Defense
earnest, elegant as a pompeian matron
supped next to me.   Much admired
for D.C. school reform   a committeewoman
of fervor
        her husband less admired
a cost product expert   hair slick as a beaver's
cold eyes instantly contracting to
the fleering public glare
        expanding
in the subterranean
warrens where he like a children's
animal tail
        disappeared around
this or that pentagonal corner

leaving the subaltern mice & moles
a-quiver to their nose hairs with
puritan anangke   O how
(wail) quite measure up?

Fridays the pentagon prayer room was crowded

In the postprandial mellow summer dark (quote)
"Mississippi is Vietnam.   When a people
reneges on joining the civilized world
you send in troops."
        Providence has assigned
sons and daughter to the estimable pair.
My poem concerns
the death of children.

Courage

The prison horn like a flatulent pachyderm
summons prisoners
to factory work; top pay 46c per hour;
cable assemblies for missiles.
Some take courage now and again
to fart back;
the majority shuffle along in the great
flatfoot track.
The law strikes at the living marrow;
big virtue, small returns.
See
in defeated eyes, the big booty lugged
up the wrong bloody end
of Big Sister.
The horn blows and blows; rage,
defeat, raw loss.
The prisoners pass
nature's reversal, up and into
Black Maria's ass.

This Is About Prayer

How do you pray in prison?
Quarrels, breakups, frenzies
A bad day spills over, or it is "introduced."
His Impenetrability, a being
Of fits and starts, fury, depredation: finally, we hope,
Of mercy.

So, as we hope, are we.
The juxtaposition
Nay the mutual penetration of two such wills
His, mine,
Is not a simple yinyang, an analogy
Drawn from, shored up by nature.
It is mutually, ritually wounding.
There is blood on the doorpost
Of some dwellings I know.
But the beings within do not exude
The rancor and heat of an animal hutch.
No.   They are golden fish bloodied
In the uphill rapids
Wherein they make love and die.
All this is, to the believing mind,
Admissible and sign.

Temptations

Middle age,
midterm prison.   Nowhere to go,
nowhere to come from; fed up with the clutch of man;
eternal stereotypes eternally herding; as in a vast
hecatomb, a city dump.
Brain lapse, anomie, money game.
The fine point of hell must be:
the exhausted stare,
the rifled
genetic bank.

Though hell pack them in like a Grand
Central, God or Satan search the blank mob
forever, the day after –
for what?   a face
Majesty or Travesty could make
any but mob scenes of, or body counts, or claims and
counter claims; *someone owns you!*
The fine point
of this unreal estate; courts, torts, writs and tears –
love that leash or lash!   someone owns me!

E contra, I invoke the Holy Spirit for a particular
straightening of knees, the return to breast
of red meat for rotten, a setting forth of brothers across
fifty states of dementia praecox;
Come!   choose, be chosen!

A Day's Work in the Clinic

I stand at the dentist's chair
hosing down
the havoc of his pincers
slow   slow
then a wider arc
he draws
the newborn tooth   into light of day
Another day
another bloody day
root   limb   blind as bone
stillborn as a tooth

A Prisoner Rations His Memories, 1 Per Day

A year ago this autumn   Tom Byers
one evening around the wine:
We're going to plant
for that suicide boy Fred   a green spruce

and did, Saturday.   Then the Daly hellion
broke like an egg   a midnight drag race
Tom took his shovel in hand again
better than Shakespeare's

fool   knowing autumn
as autumn does   its uses
My father's death came

that November
a 3rd tree
a free gesture   Tonight in prison
I break that wine glass
thanking
the soil that springs
locks   death   remembrance free

Come to Think of It, Hospital Is Another Working Metaphor for This Place

Fordham Hospital, open ward, years gone
I bent above the cot of a dying woman.
   Her eyes milky with encroaching death,
clear water glazed with ice, on a cold twilight
   the dead cold nears, water shrinks at the edges.
The bed sheet stiff, belly to shoulder, with her blood.
   Wearily, half submerged in that icy pall –
"The stitches broke in the night, I am dying."
   Factual: a weather report from the ravaged land and sea
of her life.
   A young priest unused
to the uses of silence, close to tears,
   what could I summon?   God's mercy?
   A weak gesture, her groan
   waved Him (and me) aside,
a malodorous fly in that foul place: "Don't speak to me of that;
the pain, the pain!" . . .

   Every morning I mount
twenty unbroken metallic steps to the prison hospital.
   Twice a day, morning and night
the sick call lines up.   30 prisoners or so
   pass muster under the eye
of the beefy ox administrator, his
   short horned head
wired for beeps of phony pain.
   He tosses them right and left –
to relief, to oblivion.
   Oblivion: "Say there where's yer copout?"
Relief: a high, a pill.
A wide-screen pneumatic empty-brained
   grade C drive-in flick
Transfiguring   transubstantiating
   To visual spurts, spurious bliss –
      prison, hospital
A piss stained rotting tenement wall

Indelibly daubed
"abandon hope . . . "

Guard

When did we add it, who added "economic" to "man"?
    destructive, cancerous, an appendage,
e.g., the guard who might be a man
    turns furtive, lopes like a stinking jackal across the icy
                                                    compound
answering the "goon squad" signal.
    I reel, seeing visions, surreal.
He kisses his little daughter tenderly
    or honors (religious man) flesh of Christ
with resounding thwacks on a prisoner's bones.

    Guard, you used to be: epitaph.
Used to be fairly a man, chatted with us, shifting feet in the cold,
    trusted for his smile.
Now he follows a cascade of green paper like falling of starlight;
    the goon squad beckons him
a deceptive mirage of money.
    He will grind men to a meat, has to.
His jaw turns on the prospect
    like a millstone, prisoners sweating beneath.

Newborn daughter at home, fervor, dollars, overtime;
    he sweats and freezes, hot as an inquisitor's crotch,
sizzles in the snow like the hoofprints of hell.
    He crosses the yard, a flash of winter lightning
Zeno's arrow; perpetually, geometrically pared
    never to strike home.

At home that tender child
weeps the day long;
he, schizoid
a heaven or hell hound
makes love there, but elsewhere
'gainst us
alas
war.

Off Off Off Way Off Broadway

Sorrowfully   helplessly   after the cultural event
   the decent faced people   tears on their faces
   in a pall of silence   conscience honed
     by words   by music
     music and words
       depart
death   horror   ring them around
   they part one from another
(nudity   bare bones   the death they shared
         momentarily)
They will gaze at their children
   helpless for thought of those distant children
The sweet trap life closes its jaws
! BONES   BONES   RAGS   RAGS!   the huckster cries
silks and satins rot in the street   a shroud

Strip Mining

Today they ordered the cell walls stripped of all pictures.
A Lieut. whose face resembles a boiled tattoo stamped in the
7th circle of hell
gave the order to a subaltern, transmitted down & down.
Down then.   A news photo of Ho, his last years, hand raised in
a cupping

lotus gesture, face a concentrated soul

a monk bending over a flower

children's faces from the People's Peace Treaty

Merton: that cool brusque cavalier's glance at the
world: No sale

The cutoff for prisoners is a severe one; they are forbidden
ancestors
and posterity

The crumpled faces lie in a disposal can somewhere; like a ditch
at My Lai

the walls, blank glassy intestinal green, grin at me like all the
carnivores of creation.

You might long for a crucifix to push back the space, divide so
foul and nightmarish a universe in quadrants; one green slice
of hell to the church, one to the state, one to the real estate
industry, one to the arms race.

I could then throw dice at the foot and assign relative punish-
ments by way of vertical land grants to the self-doomed;
sludge, befouled shorelands, strip mines, trees felled in their
prime, oil slicks; what a ruined earth was mixed in the bowl
of the brain to paint that wall!

so a man knows himself, imprisoned behind that color which is the pukehued mockery of hope;   a green putrefaction glittering back at him

the universe a blank wall painted the color of violated hope – climb its face and perish.

A riddle
over the wall one sees beetling the enormous insect, the 8th plague, his pincers awaiting the unlucky escapee. He will behead him like a horse fly, cutting off his cry of victory, as a madman snips the head of a flower in its glory, idly, for revenge

I stand there, the blank wall is filthy with bloodstained ghosts like a cave of bats over the bloated body of a votive cow. They crowd in, events   news   the last edgy idiocy of the smoky mind   feverish with lust to possess the brain of the believer

My ikons were exorcists; they held the stinking spirits at bay.

whose shadow has fallen on that wall?

whose tears and seed misspent have stained that bed, the metaphoric blood of the warrior forbidden conquest or progeny?

THE WALL   THE WALL   the imprisoned soul shouts.   the shout ricochets like a bullet striking adamant

night.   I slip my sight   from the glass case of animal skin

my feet ascend thin air

DANIEL BERRIGAN   110

A Piece of Advice to a Young Prisoner

When they own your smile, I reminded
The next man in the stripsearch line
They own your balls.   Nothing in the
Constitooshun requires handing over
That silk purse to the anti-
Ecologicals.   GIMME growls the
mercenary paw.   IN A SOW'S EAR growl
Back.   It might not be gracious but
By God it's clear, as Confucius say.
And where soul, grit and growl are
In the breech, the bag,
You'd best be clear or
J. Edgar's leer
Will hitch up
In dishonor of your
Broke and entered
Crotch
A big notch.

Reading the Poems of Ho

That cheerful attentiveness!
I am ashamed for my flaccid mind
that draws neither strength nor healing
from the springs of the world.
Prison; a 6-sided airless box, jerry built
Box, boxed, dimensions of death.

Yet today
earth burned like a bush
after a scourging night storm.
Midafternoon
a hawk, a cinquefoil, arose in the blue, straight up
at the east wall.   He drank mid-distance
into his arched bonfire bones.
Torch, torch bearer, time's daemon.   Below
the slow animal earth, lifting of prisoner's heads.

Come, Dear Reader, Stand Breathless Before This Blinding Logic

I may be forgiven the reflection; *medicine is politics.*
I had rather stretch out on my iron cot & phase out
before ever again
needles or neutralizers
of Doctor Niteshade.
The confucian logic imminent to *"don't get sick in prison"*
must be enlarged to: *"don't get sick in America."*
Events introduce the dicta 1 to another like the
2 sweaty palms of priest and mortician, meeting with blind
vermicular logic
over the cemetery fence
where I or mayhap you, cher lecteur
for real
play dead

Insanity

1.
Practically everyone goes insane here
according to William Carlos Williams' just prognosis.
The catalogue is thick as an old Sears Roebuck teaser;
insanity of the backbone (razorback, Nazi)
insanity of the buttocks (the prisoner as insect; squash!)
insanity of the crotch (nutcracker mania)
also of the forearm (the reach of justice; python long as)
of the fingers (the enemy, he is ours)
yes, of the bloodstream, juices, forethought, lobes.
Who can know the hour of onslaught?
a slavish greenish detour of the snail,
impeachment of laughter;
the sweetest tempers go under, gently,
a drowning of harmless land creatures.

2.
One child took their worst;
they won   they won
(his slender resources
a guitar   5 or 6 songs
and Mary
that quattrocento oval
stilling the air around
as still air surrounds
an ikon   as prayer stills
upstart passion)
heaven
flung
root and flower
to hell
died there

3.
Like scavengers on a field
where the dead

lie after mower and sower
deflower indiscriminate –
the brain shrinkers   damagers   justifiers
black bag in hand
toss in like turnips
the day's fresh kill.

4.
Insane authority; the abstract itch
of rectitude.   The cost invariably
borne elsewhere.
Lofty principles,
pomp and circumstance, like minded apes
in glittering mirrors, the thousand
manicured hands
laying ink to foolscap;
how many
must die!   blood, children rotting in ditches
always elsewhere!

5.
A satrap, his face
a shut briefcase, his case holding
like an official face, secrets, suspects,
anguish, disrepute, the lives of prisoners
he departs next month
for a prestigious compound
to study "criminology."
There in Ivy, will play
bwana of butterflies.
This is a poem about
insanity

A Hermit Thrush in Autumn, Over the Wall

1.
My cell gives on a barred window.   At night
I stretch an arm a few inches, feel on skin
rain fall, fall of first snow, the reluctant light
of a new moon.   Beyond, grasses that savage
or go under, 2 arthritic trees, a wall.
spread to your eyes my whole existence, these 18 months.

Now, a codicil for the memory –
a mysterious night bird haunting the outside dark
flitting ragged as a bat from tree to tree,
the heartbreaking, half corporeal
presence of memory.
His song filters through,
the locked face of the dead,
a key that opens eyes.

That bird!
it is not memory's illusion he sings –
listen; a proscribed savior
crucified there,
his blood ours for the asking.

2.
Night and day, that outburst!
Blind at the wall, I can only
imagine you; a shadow
of shadow, east of the sun
west of the moon.
And 7 seas lie between and
7 lockups . . .
Was the divine will ever more clear
that of the living
disposes?   God the Father
rampaging
from a bullhorn: *die here!*

3.
You repeat your phrase and
phantasmagoric riches
skein out & over the wall
like the unwinding
of gold foil from a sage's
mouth (message
decoded later, later when
amaze has passed and
the quotidian heart resumes its
plod toward the heap
and hole wherein, sign and hook and
crook, we are bidden
lie low, be at length
still and at length)

4.
That burst, as though the molten core of the world
were made of music, a crevasse opened
every 10 minutes or so, a watery jet
soared up,
feathered away in the wind.
Conjure too, a lazar house,
the dispirited sick on litters, hope vanished –
then
that momentary lifting of the world

Strange, we are deprived in every sense,
yet every sense more alive
in denial; 5 appetites, 5 avenues of hunger,
badly served by hollow chatter,
waste and wear;
Well, we are prisoners,
Numbered and tagged like the human meat of Attica,
the human beef shoved
into the icy drawers of the morgue

each with a tag obscenely dangling from its toe.
Birth to death, our reprobate estate
made clear to us, to church
and state
and all ships at sea.

Only –
it is not clear, God damn it!
Damn any God
shoving like a hack's hard on
the dogma up our ass.   Unclear, unclear!
Our heads ring
like liberty bells – belfries wherein lurk and dart
random fits, starts, survivals, lightnings behind clouds
weightless moons, faces under those moons,
choking grief, unexplained relief–

my list is long, brother, as
the year
that drains us like a wound, unacknowledged
as mortal, as draining, as it is –
nevertheless
out of which peers as from
nature's cicatrice
the bloody wide fish eyes of the near born.

5.
That bird is listed too; pure grief.
He sings in the darkness as I write
as he sings in the noon of yesterday and tomorrow,
his text a Rosetta stone, self-translated
mystery-haunted, Plato's
mind's cave;
Look, I fly straight from the world's core of music
I come, the world's messenger and metaphor.
As the world is my messenger and metaphor,

upbearing and upborne.
Look, your prison strips from you, only
what is not yours
proxy or parasitic to your soul.

6.
What odds will you give?
the phiz of that mordant persister,
that fleecing charmer?
9 to 1 he's a hirsute Jesus —
ragged as sin, whistling through his fingers
hoping
out of 750 fat cats —
their bellies force filled with buckshot —
one leapfrogging desecrater,
deserter, from the
Jewish Defense League or the Roman Catholic Curia
will jump over the wall into the Movement
which up to now, truth told, consists of
1 'bo
dressed like a bird
or vice versa
who whistles or farts
day after night
through Danbury keyhole
THE FIRST GREAT
COMMAND.

7.
Little man, little bird
piping
like Blake's boy
flute, throat frail as glass —
turn, turn the page.
Toward the 6th hour
the big gods in black

leather jackets
won out.
They nailed Blake's boy
blond poll
blue eyes and all
to a barn door,
in his dishonor
held an orgy there.
Toward the 9th hour
revved up and
were gone.

Foreboding, Harrisburg

An enormous encompassing weakness
wells up in my guts.
A death penalty, the long constricting months.
Spirit, unable to break free,
loiters, fails (prison within prison)
malfunctions, fades like a rose
touched by a finger of slime
freeloading loathsomely.
Tonight, a parting of leprous waters,
pain within formless pain –
thought of Philip, thought of the coming trial,
fate set by that
faceless fisherman
who summer long
from the many branched waters
plucks the choicest fruits –
lands
panting, walleyed
bloodflecked –
who?

This Is about Chickens, Pigs, Children, Nightingales and a Cathedral

Sometimes it seems to me
David and the other resisters
   like fireflies in a graveyard
exist only to prophesy
   the potential of those spare parts
      – seeds, weeds, fluff in the air –
nature in her profligate
   goodness, tosses aside
to enrich the common earth; to ensure, against random tosses
   chancy weather, a new season after all.

I wandered out of house one winter night
   along Cornell roads
to end, sitting like a landlocked
   polar bear, in a crest of snow
toppling its wave against a pine grove.
   The winter birds flocked there; the moon's
lamp, held high,
awakened them.   It was a crude
mimicry of nightingales
   I heard, keeping the death-watch
one May night in Burgundy, '54.   An old peg-legged priest in a
   skull cap,
      chugged about town for years, asthmatic
jutjawed, in an unimaginable
   3-wheeled jalopy, to mock terror
of chickens, pigs, children.
   Now, at some length, gustily,
he was shuddering to a stop.
   I paced and prayed under a peacock spread
of resurrection moon.   The nightingales
   took up their cry, tree to tree, across the town.   Unbearable
      plaint, death cry or birth.
He died
   under that fretwork of sound, whose calcination

– the old time-drenched abbey church –
  stood, listened, alight, its own
consummation, *son et lumière*. And his

A Visitor Awaits the Prisoner

You've got to hear that mechanical
ass or angel trumpeting; BERRIGAN 23742 YOU
                                        GOTTA VISIT!
It rends the cell houses
in open summer, a mad circus dog
breaking the fiery barrier.
That voice's got no choices.
As if one whispered
shamefaced in paraplegic ears –
look mom, no hands,
feet, eyes, (balls even).

For the accession of the iron mongrel
to the rickety throne, the voice must be unconnected.
No brain box, attentive (say)
to the eloquent ignorance
of some young Socrates, hell-bent on manhood
savior potentially of the god-and-man damned
state. Better therefore, equivalently
dead, i.e., under lockup.

In place of manhood's precious filament and fuel bag –
Keys, their death rattle in the yard. How many points
of possession under law?
The hack, a nation state
bestrides the world.
Hear
that rehabilitating catechetic, one time more;
bellows the dog god; *priest, punk, now*
who made the world?